I'm good at

Dancing

Eileen Day

Raintree

www.raintreepublishers.co.uk
Visit our website to find out more information about **Raintree** books.

To order:
☎ Phone 44 (0) 1865 888112
📄 Send a fax to 44 (0) 1865 314091
💻 Visit the Heinemann Bookshop at **www.raintreepublishers.co.uk** to browse our catalogue and order online.

First published in Great Britain by Raintree, Halley Court, Jordan Hill, Oxford OX2 8EJ, part of Harcourt Education.
Raintree is a registered trademark of Harcourt Education Ltd.

© Harcourt Education Ltd 2003
First published in paperback in 2004
The moral right of the proprietor has been asserted.

Editorial: Nick Hunter and Diyan Leake
Design: Michelle Lisseter
Picture Research: Alan Gottlieb and Amor Montes de Oca
Production: Lorraine Hicks

Originated by Dot Gradations
Printed and bound in China by South China Printing Company

ISBN 1 844 21501 6 (hardback)
07 06 05 04 03
10 9 8 7 6 5 4 3 2 1

ISBN 1 844 21508 3 (paperback)
08 07 06 05 04
10 9 8 7 6 5 4 3 2 1

British Library Cataloguing in Publication Data
Day, Eileen
Dancing. – (I'm good at)
792.8
A full catalogue record for this book is available from the British Library.

Acknowledgements
The publishers would like to thank the following for permission to reproduce photographs: Corbis/Michael St. Maur Sheil, **18**; Corbis/Owen Franken, **5**; Getty Images/Stone, **12**; Getty Images/Taxi, **20**; Heinemann Library/Brian Warling, **22, 24**; Heinemann Library/Robert Lifson, **11, 13, 15, 22**; International Photobank/Peter Baker, **17, 23** (tartan); Mark E. Gibson, **10, 23** (musical); Photo Edit/Bonnie Kamin, **19**; PhotoEdit/Michael Newman, **4**; PhotoEdit/Myrleen Ferjuson Cate, **21**; PhotoEdit/Tony Freeman, **9, 22, 23** (taps); Scenic Ireland, **19**; Scottish Viewpoint, **16**; Stock Boston/Bob Daemmrich, **6, 23** (ballet); Stock Boston/Rhoda Sidney, **14, 23** (costume); Unicorn Stock Photos/Aneal Vohra, **8**; Visuals Unlimited/D. Yeske, **7**.

Cover photograph reproduced with permission of Bubbles Picture Library.

Every effort has been made to contact copyright holders of any material reproduced in this book. Any omissions will be rectified in subsequent printings if notice is given to the publishers.

Some words are shown in bold, **like this**.
They are explained in the glossary on page 23.

Contents

What is dancing?

Dancing is moving your body to a beat.

It is moving your body in a special pattern.

There are many kinds of dances.

The different moves in a dance are called **steps**.

What is ballet?

Ballet is dancing that tells a story.

This ballet is about a dream.

You can go to a ballet class.

You can practise ballet **steps** at home.

What is tap?

Tap dancing is using your feet to make sounds.

You have **taps** on your shoes that make a noise.

Different **steps** make different sounds.

Some steps are loud and some steps are soft.

What is jazz?

Jazz is dance that you often see in shows and **musicals**.

Jazz dancing has many **steps**.

A teacher can show you how to do jazz steps.

You can show the steps to your parents!

What is folk dancing?

Folk dances are dances from different countries.

They are danced the same as they were a long time ago.

There are special **costumes** for some folk dances.

Some folk dances are danced in circles.

What is African dancing?

African dancing is moving to the beat of a drum.

Some African dancers wear special **costumes**.

In African dancing you jump.

You shake your body and move your feet.

What is Highland dancing?

Highland dancing comes from Scotland.

Each dance tells a story.

kilt

Highland dancers wear a type of skirt called a kilt.

Kilts and socks are made of **tartan**.

What is Irish dancing?

Irish dancing is a kind of dance called **step** dancing.

Step dancers only move their feet and legs.

Irish dancers must keep their bodies straight.

They work hard to jump high.

How do I feel when I dance?

When you dance, you feel happy.

Sometimes it feels like you can fly.

It is fun to dance with your friends.

Quiz

Can you match the right shoes with the dancer?

Look for the answer on page 24.

 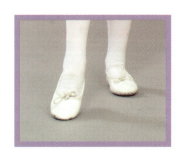 

Glossary

ballet
dance with steps and movements that tells a story

costume
clothes worn in a certain country or at a certain time in the past

musical
a film or play in which there is lots of singing and dancing

steps
pattern of moves of the feet in a dance

tartan
cloth made of wool with a pattern of stripes

taps
metal discs on the bottom of dancing shoes that make a noise against the floor

Index

Answer to quiz on page 22

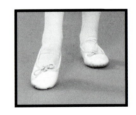